Paganism in Christian Holidays

*Did Christianity Borrow
From Other Belief Systems?*

Some Other Titles From New Falcon Publications

Aha! The Sevenfold Mystery of the Ineffable Love —Aleister Crowley
Aleister Crowley and the Treasure House of Images
   —J.F.C. Fuller, Aleister Crowley, Lon Milo DuQuette and Nancy Wasserman
Aleister Crowley's Illustrated Goetia, Sex Magic, Tantra & Tarot:
An Insider's Guide to Robert Anton Wilson —Eric Wagner
Ask Baba Lon —Lon Milo DuQuette
Bio-Etheric Healing —Trudy Lanitis
Diary of the Antichrist —David Cheribum
Enochian Sex Magic and How To Workbook
   —Aleister Crowley, Lon Milo DuQuette and Christopher S. Hyatt, Ph.D.
Enochian World of Aleister Crowley —DuQuette and Aleister Crowley
Info-Psychology, Neuropolitique, The Game of Life, What Does WoMan Want?
   —Timothy Leary, Ph.D.
Nonlocal Nature: The Eight Circuits of Consciousness —James A. Heffernan
Numbers Their Meaning and Magic Vol. I & II, Zodiacal Symbology Book 1 & 2
   —Isidore Kozminsky
on What is —Ja Wallin
Rebellion, Revolution and Religiousness —Osho
Rebels & Devils; The Psychology of Liberation—Edited by Christopher S. Hyatt, Ph.D.
Reichian Therapy: A Practical Guide for Home Use —Dr. Jack Willis
Shaping Formless Fire, Seizing Power, Taking Power
Secrets of Western Tantra: The Sexuality of the Middle Path
Dogma Daze —Christopher S. Hyatt, Ph.D.
Steamo Goes to Havana, The Social Epidemic of Child Abuse
   —Michael Miller, M.Ed., M.S., Ph.D.
The Illuminati Conspiracy: The Sapiens System —Donald Holmes, M.D.
The Magick In The Music and Other Essays —Stephen Mace
The Philosophy of Numbers, Vol. I & II, Nature's Symphony **Mrs. L. Dow Balliett**
The Psychopath's Bible —Christopher S. Hyatt, Ph.D., and Jack Willis
The Secret Inner Order Rituals of the Golden Dawn —Pat Zalewski
The Way of the Secret Lover Taboo: Sex, Religion & Magick
   —C. Hyatt, Ph.D., and Lon DuQuette
The Why, Who, and What of Existence —Vlad Korbel
Undoing Yourself With Energized Meditation and Other Devices
Woman's Orgasm: A Guide to Sexual Satisfaction
   —Benjamin Graber M.D., and Georgia Kline-Graber, R.N.

Other Titles by J. Marvin Spiegelman, Ph.D.

A Modern Jew in Search of Soul
Buddhism and Jungian Psychology
Catholicism and Jungian Psychology
Hinduism and Jungian Psychology
Mysticism, Psychology and Oedipus - A Small Gem
Protestanism and Jungian Psychology
Psychotherapy and Religion at the Millennium and Beyond
Psychotherapy as a Mutual Process
Reich, Jung, Regardie & Me - The Unhealed Healer
Rider, Haggard, Henry Miller & I - The Unpublished Writer
Sufism, Islam and Jungian Psychology
The Knight - A Small Gem
The Nymphomaniac
The Quest - Further Adventures in the Unconscious
The Tree of Life - Paths in Jungian Individuation
The Wisdom of J. Marvin Speigelman Vol. I - Selected Writings
The Wisdom of J. Marvin Speigelman Vol. II - Psychology and Religion

Other Titles by Dr. Israel Regardie

A Garden of Pomegranates
A Practical Guide to Geomantic Divination - A Small Gem
Attract and Use Healing Energy - A Small Gem
Be Yourself - A Guide to Relaxation and Health
Ceremonial Magic
Dr. Israel Regardie's Definitive Work on Aleister Crowley,
  The Eye In The Triangle
Healing Energy, Prayer and Relaxation
How To Make and Use Talismans - A Small Gem
Israel Regardie's The Foundations of Practical Magick
My Rosicrucian Adventure
Mysticism, Psychology and Oedipus - A Small Gem
Practical Magick - A Small Gem
Teachers of Fulfillment
The Art and Meaning of Magic - A Small Gem
The Body-Mind Connection, A Path to Well-Being - A Small Gem
The Complete Golden Dawn System of Magic
The Complete Golden Dawn System of Magic Book 1 - Ltd. Edition
The Complete Golden Dawn System of Magic Book 2 - Ltd. Edition
The Complete Golden Dawn System of Magic - The Black Edition
The Eye in the Triangle: An Interpretation of Aleister Crowley
The Golden Dawn Audio CDs, Vol. 1, Vol. 2, and Vol. 3
The Legend of Aleister Crowley
The Magic of Israel Regardie
The Middle Pillar
The Philosopher's Stone
The Portable Complete Golden Dawn System of Magic
The Tree of Life
The Wisdom of Israel Regardie - Vol. I
  Selected Introductions, Prefaces and Forewords
The Wisdom of Israel Regardie - Vol. II
  Selected Essays and Commentaries
The Wisdom of Israel Regardie - Vol. III
  Selected Articles, Introductions, Prefaces and Forewords
What You Should Know About the Golden Dawn
Wilhelm Reich, His Theory And Techniques
Aha! (Dr. Israel Regardie and Aleister Crowley)
Roll Away The Stone/The Herb Dangerous
  (Dr. Israel Regardie and Aleister Crowley)

MANY OF OUR TITLES AVAILABLE ON KINDLE!
Please visit our website at http://www.newfalcon.com

Copyright © 2024 New Falcon Publications

All rights reserved. No part of this book,
in part or in whole, may be reproduced, transmitted,
or utilized, in any form or by any means, electronic or mechanical,
including photocopying, recording, or by any information storage
and retrieval system, without permission in writing
from the publisher, except for brief quotations
in critical articles, books and reviews.

ISBN 13: 978-156184-526-0
ISBN 10: 1-56184-526-4

New Falcon Publications First Edition 2024

The paper used in this publication meets the minimum requirements
of the American National Standard for Permanence of
Paper for Printed Library Materials Z39.48-1984

Printed in USA

NEW FALCON PUBLICATIONS
2046 Hillhurst Avenue
Los Angeles, California 90027
www.newfalcon.com
email: info@newfalcon.com

Paganism in Christian Holidays

*Did Christianity Borrow
From Other Belief Systems?*

A SMALL GEM
BY
J. M. WHEELER

NEW FALCON PUBLICATIONS
Los Angeles, California 90027, U.S.A.

CONTENTS

PAGE

CHAPTER ONE	LENT	1
CHAPTER TWO	EASTER	23
CHAPTER THREE	MAY DAY and WHITSUNTIDE	59
CHAPTER FOUR	CHRISTMAS	71

CHAPTER ONE
LENT

"Who can believe with common sense
 A bacon slice gives god offence;
 Or, how a herring hath a charm
 Almighty vengeance to disarm?
 Wrapt up in majesty divine
 Does he regard on what we dine?"

Dean Swift,

"A very ancient and fish-like smell, a kind
 not of the newest."–"*Tempest,*" Act ii, sc.3.
"La carcel y la quaresma para los
 pobres es hecha."*

Spanish Proverb

---

* Prison and Lent are suitable to the poor.

One of the main roots of religion is belief in the return of ghosts. Dreams and visions are largely accountable. Since fasting is a means of producing nervous disorder and morbid exaltation which leads to ghost-seeing, it has a prominent place in all early religions and also in the great faiths that have continued the practices and superstitions of early man. Dr. E. B. Tylor remarks: "Among the strongest means of disturbing the functions of the mind so as to produce ecstatic vision is fasting, accompanied as it so usually is, with other privations, and with prolonged solitary contemplation in the desert or the forest." The wild hunter often has to undergo involuntarily the effects of such a life for days and weeks together, and in this condition comes to see visions, and to talk with phantoms which are to him visible personal spirits. The secret of this intercourse thus learnt, he has but to reproduce the cause to renew the effects.

Fasting is an important rite among North American Indians. Long and rigorous abstinence from food is enjoined on boys and girls from a very early age. Like other now objectionable rites, this practice was rooted in stern necessity. To be able to fast long became an enviable distinction. Forty days seems to have been a very general maximum, enjoined in ancient rites of initiation and still carried out by the Yezidis of Kurdistan. Lent represents the hardest period of the year, when in hunting-life game was scarcest, with pastoral people kids and lambs were yet unborn, and even with agriculturists winter stores threatened to give out. During these fasts particular attention is paid to dreams. What one sees and experiences at this time is regarded as revelation. Dr. Tylor gives numerous instances from various nations.

Spiritually seeking revelatory dreams with the aid of fasting.

So thoroughly is the connection between fasting and spiritual intercourse acknowledged by the Zulus that they have a saying,

"The continually stuffed body cannot see secret things." They have no faith in a fat prophet. The Pythia of Delphi fasted for inspiration. Hindu yogis have a like probation. Even the physician, Galen, remarks that fasting dreams are the clearest. All the saints of the Catholic Church practised fasting, and saw their visions of heaven and hell, angels and devils, when in that condition.

Lent comes from the old Teutonic word *Lens*, meaning spring. In ancient times the

Pythia was the name of the high priestess of the Temple of Apollo at Delphi. She served as its oracle and was known as the Oracle of Delphi. She held a unique position in ancient Greek religion. She fasted for inspiration before receiving her messages.

new year commenced in spring, when the sun entered the sign of Aries. All ancient peoples regarded the spring as a period of new life. Much religion, indeed, is founded on a presumed analogy between the life of man and the course of the seasons. In its lowest efforts it consisted of charms to alter the course of nature to suit human wants. Some survival of this appears in our prayers for rain and fine weather in the Book of Common prayer. The expulsion of evils, or demons presumed to be their cause, formed a large part of old religion, in which mystery, medicine and magic were bound together. The priest is the modern survivor of the mystery-man, medicine-man, and magician, and his prayers are the modern survival of savage incantations. Devils were sometimes driven off like wild beasts, by yells and

The priest is the modern survivor of the medicine-man, medicine-woman and magician.

Ringing the old year out and the new year in is an old tradition.

noises. Fireworks in the dull season represented the attempt to drive off the demons of darkness and bring the angels of light, or sometimes these demons were expelled by clappers, horns or ringing bells. In our custom of ringing the old year out and the new one in we preserve a pleasant survival of this superstition. Fasting was found an efficacious method of dealing with some of these demons–such, we may suppose, as had their origin in intoxication, over-feeding, and fever. Christ says of a devil his disciples could not exorcise, "this kind goeth not out but by prayer and fasting." The end of the year, the period preceding spring, was the general time for getting rid of evil spirits, and to make a fresh start in life freed from their malignant influences, as the new vegetation rises freed from the frosts of winter. This time was indeed that of the temptation by the devil; the Christ of the new life having to conquer its own passions and then overcome the temptations of the devil. A period of forty days was set for this struggle. Moses, Elijah and Christ all fast for that time. It is notable that Milton in his *Paradise Regained*, like the Buddhists in their story of the conflict of Gautama with the tempter Mara, makes this initiation the most important item in his hero's career.

Gautama with tempter Mara.

Shrove Tuesday, the day of shriving, when our ancestors used to humble themselves and confess their sins to prepare for Lent, is the survival, now only in name, of the Pagan preparation for the expulsion of sins; and on Good Friday (the last Friday

Hot-cross-bun

in Lent), when nature is supposed to be at its deepest point of mourning–the darkest hour before the dawn– we take the sacramental hot-cross-bun as a sign that our redeemer, who symbolizes the sun and his fruits in vegetative nature, has passed over the barriers of death, and will return with new life, joy, and gladness to the earth. In Lent, marriages are abandoned, mourning dresses are still considered appropriate; and Easter would not be Easter to many a provincial lassie did it not bring with it new clothes as a sign that nature was freshly arraying herself; the fasting, clothes, and feasting being all charms symbolical of the life of nature.

Top-whipping, cock-shying, and cock-fighting, were ancient sports at this season. The first is a charm to accelerate the revolution of the seasons; the cock too was used in various sports, and as a sacrifice, because it was supposed, since it announced the dawn of day, to announce also the dawn of spring.

The object of fasting in Lent is to overcome the devil of winter with all the privations, ills and aches attendant on his train.
Rooster at dawn

It was also found conducive to health and good morals. The man who could abstain, did something his fellows found difficult. Hence abstinence has ever been associated with ideas of sanctity. Hindus, Chinese, Jews, and Mohammedans, all have their fasts that are supposed to make atonement for sins committed, and to predispose for a closer adherence to the rules of right living. Why Mohammedans keep Friday sacred, and why on *dies Veneris* the Catholics eat fish, may be found explained in my *Bible Studies*.

The ordinance of fasting, or rather fish-eating, with symbolic egg-sauce, on Friday, and for the forty days of Lent, should convince any misguided sceptic that our divine religion was instituted by fishermen.

Catholic tradition of eating fish on Fridays during Lent.

Jesus Christ, who told his disciples that he would make them fishers of men—and they have been trout-ticklers and flat-catchers, after the loaves and fishes, ever since—was himself, as the early Fathers said, the great *Ichthus*, the fish *par excellence*, who came by water, walked on the water, and did its miracles on the shores of the sea of Galilee,

The miracle of fish and loaves.

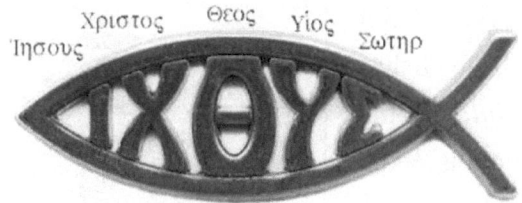

The symbol for Ichthus

like any dolphin or delphic oracle. Like the Babylonian Oannes, he was at once man, god, and fish too. Jahveh's rival, Dagon, also, was a god who, like the mermaids, was half human and half fish.[1]

In the Talmud the Messiah is called Dag, the fish, while Vishnu, one of the Trinity of India, has as his astronomical symbol the fish, and was incarnated in fish form. Tertullian says, in the beginning of third

---

[1] Morgan Kavanagh, in his curious work on the *Origin of Language and Myth*, Vol. I., p. 277, says on I Sam. v.4: "According to the marginal note in the Bible, the word *stump* is here used instead of the *fishy part*; by which we are allowed to infer the part of Dagon which resembled a *fish* was respected. But why so? Because a fish was called after water, and water after life, of which it is a principal support; and life after the sun, the supposed author of existence, and which was anciently, as we have shown from the admission of the learned, called a Saviour. Hence a fish, though not called after *Saviour*, may have often had a name not different from the one expressing this idea."

century: "But we little fishes [*pisciuli*, as the Christians liked to call themselves], after the example of *Ichthus* [i.e., the fish, J. Christ], are born in water." St. Augustine says that Christ is *Ichthus*, for the purity of Jesus Christ is found in the word fish, "for he is a fish that lives in the midst of the waters," while Julius Africanus plainly calls Christ that "great Fish who fed from himself the disciples on the shore and offered himself as a fish to the whole world." It has been conjectured that the fish among those from Asia was taken as a type of a heavenly messenger, from the fact of fish occasionally falling from the clouds in heavy showers of rain.

Vishnu incarnated in fish form.

Some persons, with more ingenuity than archeology, have conjectured that, since there is no other way to heaven but the way of the tank, the practice of ducking believers beneath water in poly baptism gave rise to the comparison between the Christian and the fish. But the fish symbol was an ancient pre-Christian one, which came into special signification about 263 B.C., when the sun entered Pisces. *Ichthus* was a title onto only of Jesus, but of Bacchus and Horus. The Sibylline oracles, which existed long before the Christian era, contained an acrostic on the word *Ichthus*. The early Christians interpreted this as meaning Ieous CHreistos, THeou Uios Soter, Jesus Christ, the Son of God, the Saviour. Justin Martyr, the earliest Christian writer of undisputed authenticity, in the middle of the second century, appeals to the Sibyl as predicting "in a clear and patent manner, the advent of our Saviour Jesus

The astrological symbol Pisces

Christ," and Celsus soon after nicknamed the Christians "Sibyllists." Possibly what the Sibylline books predicted was simply that the equinox would pass from Aries into Pisces–from the Lamb of God into the Divine Fishes. (Gerald Massey: *Natural Genesis*, i. 454), "When the equinox passed into the sign of Pisces, the fish became the figure of the Christ on the cross. Hence the fish on the pre-Christian cross which is found in Scotland and Ireland, and the fish type which was continued whenever the reckonings were kept." He further tells us that "Horus in Egypt had been a fish from the time immemorial, and when the equinox

Egyptian God Horus as part fish.

entered the sign of Pisces, Horus, who was continued by the Gnostics, is portrayed as *Ichthus* with the fish sign over his head." Jesus said his only sign is that of Jonas, who was swallowed by a fish, or, as Kenneth Mackenzie says, "absorbed into the *Vesica Pisces*." This writer, in his *Royal Masonic Cyclopaedia*, cites Dr. Crucifix, who says: "In former days, the Grand Master of our Order used to wear a silver fish on his person." Dr. Kenealy, in the curious anonymous hodge-podge he called *The Book of God*, said (p. 240), "*the fishes* mystically signify the Initiated into the Eleusinia." In the Roman catacombs one of the most frequent symbols is the fish, generally taken as a sign that those using it were Christians, though this must be considered problematical. Everywhere in early Christian symbolism we find prominence given to the fish. It is found on gravestones, mural decorations, seals, lamps, and, indeed, whatever ingenuity could engrave or paint it. It was a private mark which indicated that the persons were of the new covenant,

Fish symbol widely used in Christian, Egyptian and Roman art.

recognizing their God under the sign of the *Ichthus*. It proved they were up to the time of day."

The Catacombs often represent fishes with loaves as a sign of abundance, connected with the good shepherd of the heavens, our lord and life-giver the sun, who turns water into wine, walks on the water, and rises from the dead. I think it quite possible that the customs and legends connected with such representations gave rise to stories of feeding multitudes with a few loaves and fishes, of the fish that so opportunely paid the taxes, and of the resurrected Lord eating broiled fish and honeycomb, and ascending skyward with this provender stowed in his interior.

Major-General Forlong (*Rivers of Life*, i. 246) says: "This fish is universally worshipped in all lands as the most fecundate of all creatures; and, where most valued, the superstitious have offered it in sacrifice to their gods, refusing to eat or injure it." While some abstained from fish, others partook of it as the sacred food, taken as a preparation for a following feast. Fish are known to be extraordinary prolific. Ancient dietetics was largely based on belief that animals noted for any peculiarity imparted their virtues to those who ate them. The use of fish in connubial feasts is still common. We may be quite sure that those who first thought it proper and pious to eat fish on Venus Day, or Friday, adhered to a more ancient faith than that which praises those who make themselves eunuchs (Matt.

xix. 12). In Japan a typical paper fish suspended over the doorway of the house where a child has been born. Let the student also note what Lajard says of the Friday worship of the Druses of Lebanon on p. 58 of his *Culte de Venus*. The Jews retain the custom of a Friday fish supper, as do religious Christians, and in especial monks and nuns, the modern *Kadeshim* (holy ones), use a fish die on *Dies Veneris*. Lenten fare is a preliminary to the celebration of the spring resurrection.

Japanese paper fish displayed to announce the birth of a child.

The most interesting feature of Lent to the antiquarian is Mid lent or Mothering Sunday. Such far-fetched explanations of this

Mothering Sunday.

title have been given, as that it comes from "Jerusalem the mother of us all" being mentioned in the epistle for the day, or from parishioners having then to visit their mother church, that I shall not scruple to connect it with the cult of Mother Goddess worshipped by the Romans on the ides of March, and also preserved in our Lady Day. As at this time of year the Great Mother conceived, it was natural that she should bring forth in nine months, vis., on December 25. Hone says (*Every Day Book*, i-358, March 14): "On this day boys went about, in ancient times, into villages, with a figure of death made of straw; from whence they were generally driven by the country people who disliked it as an ominous appearance, while

In Mesopotamia it was ISHTAR who assumed the role of Mother of the Gods and as such was also the controller of fertility and vegetation and, as such, became identified with Mother Earth. Inanna's cult of the earth synchronized with seasonal cycle in both myth and ritual where the goddess as Inanna/Ishtar..."represented the source of all generative power in nature and in mankind as the Universal Mother." (James, 1959).

Demeter, also Mother Goddess.

some gave them money to get the manikin carried off." This however was only part of another ceremony conducted by a larger body of boys from whom the death carriers were a detachment. "They carried two figures to represent Spring and Winter; the first appareled all in green, and dressed in youthful fine array; the other winter clad in moss with hair and hoar gray." The proceedings ended in a fight in which of course Spring gained a victory. In Bohemia, on the same day, young people throw a puppet called Death into the water; then the girls go into the wood, cut down a young tree and dress it up like a woman and bear it round from house to house singing "We carry Death out of the village. We bring Summer into the village." Here Summer is "Our Lady." Mothering Sunday is also called Rose Sunday, from the Pope on

Pope carrys golden rose on Rose Sunday.

this day carrying a golden rose in his hand, which he exhibits on his way to and from mass. In Seville on this day children of all ranks appear in the streets, the crowd knock at every door, repeat the cry, and conclude by sawing in two the figure of an old woman. This is said to be emblematic of Mid-Lent.

"Servants who ask of their mistresses permission to leave their duties for a few hours, consider 'It is Mothering Sunday' as quite a final argument. The only accessory

The servants enjoyed wine and frumenty (wheat pudding) for Mothering Sunday.

in connection with this institution known to me is the cake, a suspicious looking creation coated with white and embellished with pink" (*Folk-lore of Gloucestershire*, p. 20.) E. Walford says, "Cake was not the only attraction of Mothering Sunday. At the Swan Inn, Wotton-under-Edge, Gloucestershire, there was wine also for all the servants, who were at liberty to bring their friends and sweethearts, and doubtless the same custom prevailed in other houses." It was also the fashion to distribute frumenty on Mothering Sunday.

CHAPTER TWO
EASTER

"They relate that the sacred tree is cut on that day on which the sun comes to an apex of the equinoctial apsis; on the next day they go round with trumpets; on the third day the sacred ineffable fruits of the god Gallus are cut. After these are the Hilaria Feasts." —F. C. Julianus (Imperator), *De matre deorum*.

> "Thammuz came next behind,
> Whose annual wound to Lebanon allured
> The Syrian damsels to lament his fate,
> In amorous ditties all a summer's day;
> While smooth Adonis from his native rock
> Ran purple to sea, supposed with blood
> Of Thammuz yearly wounded."
> *Milton, P. L., i., 446.*

It is said that when St. Augustine landed in England, he found the Britons observing Easter in the Asiatic way. There was nothing strange in this. If an intelligent Pagan were able to revisit "the glimpses of the moon" and observe our celebrations of Good Friday and Easter, he would smile when told that the observances were in celebration of a certain Jesus who was put to death in Palestine eighteen hundred years ago, and who, on the third day, rose again. "Why," he would say in astonishment, "is not this your Spring Festival such as has been observed by every nation? How came you to hold the

Spring festivals observed worldwide.

Vernal Equinox.

anniversary of a man's death on a movable date? The man who stole the saucepan and made a new lid for it took good care that the lid fitted. But the Christian lid, put on the old Pagan saucepan, does not fit. The fact that your Easter shifts according to the phases of the moon shows it is our astronomical festival. But you say it is not a man you celebrate, but a God. Of course it is; the great god of gods, the power of revivification symbolized in every tree, and in the visible luminary, the life-giving sun, who has now crossed the vernal equinox and rises again triumphant over winter and death. Have you never

The Egyptian Osiris, Jesus, and the Syrian Tammuz.

heard how we celebrated the resurrection of Adonis, even as the Syrians did that of Thammuz, the Egyptians of Osiris? Go, read in Theocritus how those delightful gossips, Gorgo and Praxinoe, babble at the festival of the god, how they listen to his dirge, and rejoice at the decorations." Matthew Arnold says: "Adonis was the sun in his summer

Adonis

and in his winter course, in his time of triumph and his time of defeat; but in his time of triumph still moving towards his defeat, in his time of defeat still returning towards his triumph. Thus became the emblem of the power of life and the bloom of beauty, hastening inevitably to diminution and decay, yet in that very decay, yet in that very decay finding 'hope, and a renovation without end.' "[1] What does the name Easter tell us? According to Bede, and the best modern authorities, the word Easter is derived from Eostre, the Saxon goddess of the east, signifying the dawn and spring, whose festival our forefathers celebrated at this season. The Saxon *Ostre* means "to rise." Throughout the pagan world the revivification of vegetation was celebrated

Ostera, the Saxon Pagan Goddess

with festivals, which symbolized the reproductive powers of nature. The time when the

---

[1] *Pagan and Medieval Religious Sentiment: Essays in Criticism*, p. 196.

sun, passing over the vernal equinox, proclaims himself redeemer of the world from winter is naturally that of the feast of the Passover, not the mythical crossing of the Red Sea but the yearly passage of the world from the bonds of winter to the life and vigor of summer. At this season the Egyptians held a feast to Isis, and the palm was carried about as the symbol of reproductive power and triumph long ere Palm Sunday was supposed to signify the entrance of Christ into Jerusalem. Easter is probably allied to Ishtar, the Assyrian goddess of love and fecundity, who was said to have descended to hell. She is similar to the Phoenician Astarte and Ashtoreth of the

Passover

Temple of Isis

Zidonians for whom Solomon built the Mount of Corruption (2 Kings xxiii. 13) at Jerusalem. The Syrian God Thammuz or Adonis, was first mourned and then believed to have risen from the dead. The same fable was related to the Egyptian God Osiris. These gods all represented the reproductive power of nature, and were celebrated at spring festivals.

Palm Sunday

There is no trace of the celebration of Easter as a Christian festival in the New Testament (Acts xii. 4, is a mistranslation; *Easter* should be *Passover*), or in the writings of the apostolic fathers. Early in history of the Church we hear of two divisions of the original Salvation Army, who disputed for centuries about the time when Easter should be kept. At the end of the second century Pope Victor wrote an imperious letter to the Eastern Church commanding them to conform to the Western practice. They refused, and were stigmatized as heretics. Epiphanius tells us: "Some began the festival before the full moon week, some at the beginning, some at the middle, some at the end, thus creating a wonderful laborious confusion." At the Council of Nice, under Constantine, it was fixed, as now, on the first Sunday after the full moon which happens upon or next after the vernal equinox. As the Egyptians excelled in astronomy, the Bishop of Alexandria was appointed to give notice of Easter Day to the Pope and other patriarchs. This, however, did not ensure uniformity. We learn from St. Ambrose (Epist. 23) that in 387 the churches of Gaul kept March 21, while those of Italy postponed it to March 28, and those of Egypt a week later still, to April 5. Similar discrepancies are mentioned by Gregory of Tours in the year 577; nor did they disappear till the eighth century.

The fact of Easter being a movable feast proves its astronomical origin, and the differences among early Christians show their ignorance of the date when their godman is alleged to have burst the bonds of death. They have never even fixed the year of that extraordinary occurrence with any certainty. While the Gospels make Jesus prophesy that he would spend three days and three nights in the heart of the earth, the narratives make him to have spent only one day and two nights. According to the Synoptics, the crucifixion took place on a Friday, the first day of Passover, but according to the established principle of the Jewish calendar, the first day of the Passover never can

The tomb of Jesus.

fall on Friday. To make the crucifixion happen on the Passover is as improbable as to allege that an Irish Fenian was hanged on a Sunday. At that time there were no courts sitting, and certainly no execution could be permitted according to Jewish law. It is most unlikely that the Roman governor of Judea would so offend Jewish prejudice as to permit an execution at the time of the Paschal feast.

That the Western Church in early times celebrated the last supper on the one day and the resurrection on the next indicated that the Christian festival sprung from the old Pagan offerings of bread and wine to the sun god being mixed up with the Jewish sacrifice of the Paschal lamb, and this

Ancient and modern offerings to the Sun god.

Symbol of the sacrificial Paschal lamb.

may have led to the legend of the Lamb of God having been put to death at the time of the Passover, the period of the year when the representative sacrifice was offered to ensure the fertility of the soil.

It is difficult for Christians to realize how close was the resemblance which the rites adopted by the Church in honor of Christ's resurrection bore to those practised by the Greeks, Phoenicians, Syrians, Egyptians, Hindus, and many other nations in honour of the god of resurrection, under the names

Akhenaten honoring the sun.

of Adonis, Dionysos, Thammuz, Osiris, Krishna, etc. Godfrey Higgins in his *Anacalypsis* (ii 106) says: "We have already seen that in Hindustan and Britain the procreative power of nature as celebrated on the day of the vernal equinox by Phallic rites, Huli festivals, May poles, and April fools, and is even yet continued in these extreme points of East and West–of India and Britain.

May Day bonfire.

On the same day in Persia, the triumph of the Good over the Evil Principle took place–the triumph of Light over Darkness, of Oromasdes over Ahriman. At the same time, in Egypt, Phrygia, Syria, were celebrated the deaths and

Aztec offering to the Sun God.

The resurrection of Osiris.

resurrections of Osiris, Attys, and Adonis. In Palestine, again, we find, on the same day, the Jews celebrating their Passover, the passage of the equinox from the sign of the Bull to that of the Ram, and of the Sun from the inferior to the superior hemisphere; and, to conclude all, on this day we Christians of Europe still continue to celebrate the victory of the god Sol, known to all nations above enumerated by his different names–by us 'The Lamb of God' which taketh away the sins of the world–on Easter

Sunday, having risen to life and immortality, triumphing over the power of hell and of darkness."

The ancient Christian year began with Easter. Religious worship was celebrated by night; and the vigils continued till cock-crowing announced the birth of the new sun. Then the stillness of the midnight vigils was broken by the joyful acclamation, "The Lord is risen! The Lord is risen! The Lord is risen indeed!" Easter day was celebrated with every demonstration of joy. In the Roman Catholic Church we may see more of the Pagan element. At cock-crowing tapers are lighted. St. Peter's at Rome is illuminated, and the vicar of Christ, his vestments blazing with gold, pronounces a blessing upon the world from a high balcony at mid-day. Eusebius, in the sixth book of his "Ecclesiastical

Cock crowing at dawn.

History," chapter viii, tells us that on one occasion the early Christians were celebrating "the solemn vigils of Easter," when, to their dismay, they found that oil was wanted. Narcissus, Bishop of Jerusalem, commanded water to be brought, and this he miraculously changed into oil in order that the celebration might be duly observed. This story shows that the early Christian Easter was quite similar to the Pagan solar festival.

Saint Narcissus, Bishop of Jerusalem.

The Spring equinox was observed among all the ancient nations of the East as the beginning of the new year, and as a season of rejoicing in honour of the sun-god, and of his return to the clothe the earth with verdure, and "fill men's heart with food and gladness." He appeared then to rise triumphant over darkness and death, and to bring back life and light to the world. Hence the fabric of the sun dancing on Easter Day. The sun was said to dance because the chief or high priest who represented the sun actually did dance at this season. In Sussex Good Friday is still known as "Marble Day," because marbles were played as a sun-charm, as also were shuttle-cocks.

A rare book entitled *Recreation for Ingenious Headpieces*, published in London in 1667, contains a ballad by Sir John Suckling, in which this belief is alluded to:–

> "But Dick, she dances such a way!
> No sun upon an Easter Day,
> Is half so fine a sight."

Sir Thomas Browne says, "We shall not, I hope, disparage the resurrection of our Redeemer, if we say the sun doth not dance on Easter Day; and although we would willingly assent unto any sympathetical exaltation, yet we cannot conceive therein anything more than a tropical

On Easter Medieval clergy played ball in labyrinths, such as the one at Chartres Cathedral.

expression." In the early days of Christianity in Britain both ecclesiastics and laics used to play at ball in the churches at Eastertide. Chambers' *Book of Days* tells us how bishops and deans took the ball into the church, and at the commencement of the antiphon began to dance, throwing the ball to the choristers, after which they had refreshments, a gammon of bacon (said to be eaten in abhorrence of the Jews) being the standard dish. The Easter cakes, which in olden times the clergy presented to

A variety of Easter breads.

their parishioners, were, like Good Friday buns, also survivals of the solar worship, a sign of which so evidently remains in all our churches having their altars built to the east.

The Rev. T. D. Fosbroke, in his *British Monachism*, thus naively describes the ball dance: "A ball not of size to be grasped by one hand only, being given out at Easter, the dean and his representative began an antiphon suited to Easter Day; then, taking the ball in his left hand, he commenced a dance to the tune of the antiphone, the others dancing round hand in hand. At intervals the ball was bandied, or passed to each of the choristers. The organ played according to the dance and sport. The dancing and antiphon being concluded, the choir went to take refreshment. It was the privilege of the lord, or his *locum tenem*s, to throw the ball; even the Archbishop did it." (p. 56.)

Among significant Easter customs was that of putting out all the church fires and re-lighting them on Easter morning from a flint. In parts of Ireland great preparations were made on Easter Eve to wind up the seven penitential weeks. The cotter's wife placed a fat hen and a piece of bacon in the pot about eight or nine o'clock. At midnight the monotonous silence would be suddenly broken by the clapping of hands, laughter and uproarious merriment, combined with the cry from lusty lungs of "Out with the Lent!" The merriment continued about four hours, when each family would retire, and before break of day rise to see the sun dance, a practice not confined to rustics.

At Twickenham it was an ancient custom every Easter Day to divide two great cakes in the parish church, and distribute pieces among the young people. In 1645 it was ordained by Parliament that such a relic of superstition should cease, and that bread should instead be given to the poor of the parish. Loaves used to be thrown from the church steeple at Paddington, to be scrambled for, a practice followed in other parishes. This was a remnant of scrambling for the body of the sacrifice, as seen in the worship of Dionysus, or its distribution, as with the Meriah victim of Khonds. At the village of Islip, Northamptonshire, every Good Friday, the baker of the village receives instructions from the Vicar to make a large cross of dough containing currants. This cross is deposited in the church, and at noon on Good Friday it is cut up and distributed to the parishioners. Dr. J. G. Frazer gives many instances of the corn spirit being eaten sacramentally. Sometimes "the corn spirit is conceived as an animal, this divine animal being slain and eaten." Again, as a substitute for the real fish of the divine being, bread or dumplings are made in his image (G. B. ii. 31). Dr. Frazer suggests that the loaves in human form, baked at Aricia, were sacramental bread, and that "in the old days, when the divine King

Corn offering, and symbolic sacrifice in ancient Mexico.

of the Wood was annually slain, loaves were made in his image, like the paste figures of the gods in Mexico, and were eaten sacramentally by his worshippers." The interesting survival at Islip is one of many indications that the death and resurrection of Christ was like the death and resurrection of John Barleycorn, an emblem of the renewal of nature in the spring.

John Barleycorn

"Heaving" or "lifting" was a favorite pastime with the people of England on the Monday and Tuesday in Easter week.

English Easter custom of "Heaving".

Sometimes it was practised indoors, but more generally in the public streets. People formed into groups, and from each one "lifted" they extorted a contribution. The ceremony was incomplete without three distance elevations. The women's "heaving" day, Tuesday, was considered the most amusing. When a man was seized he was "heaved" and kissed, and forced to pay sixpence, "for leave and license to depart." The lifting or elevation was a sign of the raising of vegetative life. It was an indecent parallel of Christ being lifted up on the cross. The practice apparently prevailed among all ranks. According to Durand it was customary for wives to beat their husbands on Easter Monday, and on the following day for husbands to retaliate the chastisement upon their spouses.

In Lancashire, Cheshire, Staffordshire, and Warwickshire the "lifting" is still practised. On Easter Monday the men lift the women, and on Easter Tuesday the women lift the men.

Mr. Lyons, the Keeper of Records of the Tower of London, has given an extract from one of the rolls in his custody, which mentions a payment made to certain ladies and maids of honour for "lifting" King Edward the First on Easter Monday. The sum that "Longshanks" paid for his luxury was no trifle, for it was equal to near five hundred pounds.

Not a century ago it was customary in Durham for boys to assemble on Easter Day, and at four o'clock to scour the streets and accost every female they met with the demand, "Pay for your shoes, if you please." The shoes were carried off by force

"Pay for your shoes, if you please."

provided pence were not forthcoming, money thus obtained being either squandered at the public-houses, or divided in shares amongst the freebooters. A like privilege was claimed by the women on Easter Monday. They began earlier in the day, and attacked every male they met. If their victim wore boots which could not easily be taken off, they would seize his hat, which they would hand about from one to another, until the owner paid sixpence for its restitution. In Yorkshire it was usual to stop those who rode on horseback, and strip them of their spurs. A plan pursued in other parts was to stretch a rope across the roads and demand hack-money. These were all relics of the change in position indicated by the death of the old king of the wood and the advent of the new one. In the thirteenth century, whenever an ecclesiastic appeared in the streets between Easter and Pentecost, he was sure to be seized, and could only obtain his liberty by payment of a fine.

The most important of the old festivities, and one in a line with the ancient rites found in Congo, Korea and Africa was the appointment of a Carnival King.

Carnival King.

We read of its being practised at Lostwithiel, in Cornwall, near where the prince of Cornwall formerly resided. The freeholders of that town and manor having elected one among them as their king, he was gaily attired and gallantly mounted, with a crown on his head and a scepter in his hand, while a sword was borne before him. Attended by a large retinue of equestrians, he rode to church in solemn state, where he was met at the porch by the priest, and treated by him with much pomp and reverence.

After service was ended, the "king" repaired, with the same formality, to a house prepared for his reception, where a grand banquet was given, in keeping with the pseudo-monarch's assumed dignity. After dinner he was disrobed, and descended to his former level. (Hone, E.D. B., ii. 441). In France this pseudo-king became a court office, the king of the ribalds. His robes cost 270 francs. In Russia the court fool mounted the imperial throne and the Czar appeared before him to give an account of his actions and receive the admonition that promotion should be according to merit. In many places it was customary at this time to elect a mock ruler. At Weston near Bath a mock mayor used to be elected. At Randwich an annual revel

The Fool King.

is kept on the Monday after Low Sunday, probably the wake of the church, attended with much intemperance and ridiculous ceremonies in the choice of a mayor who is yearly elected on that day, form amongst the meanest of people. They plead the prescriptive right of ancient customs for the licence of the day and the authority of the magistrate is not able to suppress it (Rudder, *Hist. Gloucestershire*, 619). *The Gloucestershire Journal*, April 14, 1888, chronicles a mock election and says, "The office is not much sought after, but if the villagers decide upon their mayor, and he hide himself, they seek after him and thrust the honour upon him."

It is stated that as the Emperor Charles the Fifth was once passing through a village of Arragon, on Easter Day, he was accosted by a peasant who had been chosen the 'Paschal" or "Easter King," decorated with a tin crown, and a spit in his hand for a scepter. He demanded of the Emperor that he should take off his hat to him, "For, sir,"

Feast of fools.

said he, "it is *I* who am king." To which his sovereign wittily replied, "Much good may it do you, my friend: you have chosen an exceedingly troublesome employment."

It was in connection with the custom of the king abdicating for a time that we still have the custom of kings washing the feet of beggars and distributing Royal Maundy charities on Maunday Thursday, the day before Good Friday. Each year of her life Her Majesty gives two more silver pennies to one more poor man, and one more poor woman. Last year there were seventy-six men and seventy-six women. This old custom represents a commutation for the surrender of the royal life. As late as the time of James II, the king on Maundy Thursday washed the feet of so many beggars, the Emperor of Austria did so this very year. The old ceremony in England was "washing and kissing the feet of as many paupers as they were years old; after which money and food was given them out of a basket." (J. Ecclestone, *English Antiquities*, p. 317). The King was supposed to be the representative of Christ washing the feet of the apostles. In Seville the archbishop gives a splendid dinner to twelve paupers clothed gaily at the expense of their host and each is furnished with a basket to take away what they do not eat. In Rome the Pope washes the feet of thirteen priests to whom he gives a napkin and a flower.

Jesus washing the feet of disciples.

Maundy is said to be from the *maunds* or baskets which were carried in procession and from which the royal gifts were given, twelve baskets full. Possibly it is however from *mandatum*. It was also called Shere Thursday from the custom of making a sacrificial offering of hair. When the king dropped washing beggars' feet, the office was performed by the chief Almoner, who soon gave it up also.

In the old churches the Sepulchre Show was the important feature from Good Friday to Easter. Every church had a sepulchre, in which a figure of the Christ or the dead year was laid. The ceremony of

Church of the Holy Sepulchre.

watching the sepulchre was kept up in England till the Reformation. It was said the second coming of Christ would be at this period, and therefore the sepulchre was watched. Really it was the same ceremony as watching the gardens of Adonis. On Easter Day the "Resurrection at the Sepulchre" was performed, the dramatis personae being monks, clothed in habiliments suited to the character they assumed. I doubt not that some such drama was performed before the Gospels were written. The lights at the Sepulchre Show formed no trivial part of the attraction. One massive taper, called the Paschal, was lighted in each church. That at Westminster Abbey, in 1557, weighed three hundred pounds; that at Durham Cathedral was made of pure wax, square in shape,

Paschal tapers.

and extended to within half-a-dozen feet of the roof. Every church in London had a "sepulchre." Prof. J. H. Middleton tells us in Christ's College Magazine (No. 2, p. 9) how at Christ's College, Cambridge, the host and crucifix were placed on Friday in the sepulchre and guarded by living watchers; on Easter Sunday they were taken out and a solemn service performed.

Lady Morgan in her *Italy*, describes the sepulchres there as watched night and day by hundreds in deep mourning from the dawn of Holy Thursday till Saturday at mid-day when the body is supposed to rise, and the resurrection is announced by the firing of cannon, which from the preceding Thursday had been carefully tied up to protect them from the power of the devil.

The use of eggs at Easter was universal, a custom still far from extinct. Throughout the North of England, *pace*-eggs–that is, Passover eggs hardened by boiling and tinged with the juice of herbs–were wont not only to be eaten, but placed with in the

Egg dance.

fields, as though they were balls or bowls. In the Lake District, and other places, they send reciprocal presents of colored eggs to the children of families between whom any intimacy existed. Sometimes eggs were "blessed" in quantities for distribution throughout the kingdom. The form of consecration appears in the Ritual of Pope

Paul the Fifth. The Greeks also make presents of colored eggs and cakes at Easter. In Russia, a routine of extensive visiting is adopt-

Fancy decorated Easter eggs.

ed. An egg is given and exchanged at each visit. People go to each other's houses in the morning, and introduce themselves by saying "Christ is risen." The reply is, "Yes, He is risen.

At Passover, Jewish women place hard boiled eggs on a special plate.

Jewish Passover plate with egg.

Persians, also, present each other with colored eggs on the 20th of March and following days, when they hold their great festival of the solar new year. To the philosophy and theology of the Egyptians, Persians, and other ancient nations, indeed, may clearly be traced the practice of distributing and presenting eggs at Easter. Among those people, an egg was regarded as emblematic of the universe, as well as a symbol of fecundity and new life. "Dyed eggs were sacred Easter offerings in Egypt," says the folklorist, Mr. Bonwick. A festival took place in the new moon of the month Phamenoth (which, like the Jewish Nisan, began at March 8) in honour of Osiris, when painted and gilded eggs were exchanged in reference to the beginning

Persian Nowruz egg.

of things. The transference of the beginning of the year to January, has, in France been properly followed by the sending of eggs at that season. In Italy sometimes they are stained yellow, purple, red, green, or striped with various colors; sometimes crowned with paste-work, representing in a most primitive way, a hen–her body being the egg, and her pastry-head adorned with a disproportionately tall feather. These eggs are exposed for sale at the corners of the streets and bought by everybody.

The accounts of the blessings of a ship by Apuleius might almost stand for a description of the modern ceremony at Easter. "The high priest," he says, "carrying a lighted torch and an egg, and sometimes sulphur, made the most solemn prayers with his chaste lips, completely purified it, and consecrated it to the goddess."[1] It will be seen that the significant customs at Easter take us back to pre-Christian times.

---

[1] *Chambers' Encyclopedia*, article "Easter."

CHAPTER THREE
MAY DAY and WHITSUNTIDE

"I'm wunderschönen Monat Mai
Als alle Knospen sprangen
Da ist in meinem Herzen
Die Liebe aufgegangen."
　　　　　–Heine.*

---

*'Twas in the beauteous month of May
When all the flowers were springing,
That first within my bosom,
I heard love's echo ringing.."
　　　　—E. A. Bowring.

Jack in the Green.

The decoration of horses with rosettes, or an occasional "Jack in the Green," and girls with paper feathers dancing round a barrel organ, are all that remains to remind the Londoner of the old festival of May Day. When I was a youth, it was the custom to trip out early in the country to get the May dew and gather hawthorn. This old Pagan practice is not quite extinct. Shakespeare, in his *Henry the Eighth*, alludes to it, saying it is impossible to make people sleep on May morning. And who does not remember that passage in *Midsummer Night's Dream*, where Lysander appoints to meet Hermia.

> "—In that wood, a league without the town,
> Where I did meet thee once with Helena,
> To do observance to a morn of May?"

Chaucer, in his "Court of Love," tells us that early on May morning "forth goeth all the court to fetch the flowers fresh, and branch, and bloom."

To this custom of early rising Herrick alludes, in his fine pastoral on "Corinna's Going a Maying":—

> "Get up, get up, for shame; the blooming morn
> Upon her wings presents the god unshorn.
> See how Aurora throws her fair,
> Fresh-quilted colors through the air;
> Get up, sweet slug a-bed, and see
> The dew bespangling herb and tree.
>
> ******
>
> There's not a budding boy or girl, this day,
> But is got up, and gone to bring in May.
> A deal of youth, ere this, is come
> Back, and with white-thorn laden, home."

And in Tennyson's "May Queen"—

> "You must wake and call me early, call me early, mother dear."

Early rising was but a survival of a vigil in which the fun was kept up through the night. Stubbes, a Puritan writer of Queen Elizabeth's time, in his Anatomie of Abuses," published in 1585, says" "Against May, Whit-Sunday, or other time, all the young men and maids, old men and wives, run gadding about over night to the woods, groves, hills, and mountains, where they spend all the night in pleasant

Birch branches were brought home and decorated.

pastimes; and in the morning they return, bringing with them birch and branches of trees, to deck their assemblies with all; and no meruaile for there is a great Lord present amongst them as superintendent and Lord of their sports–namely, Satan, prince of hell. But the chiefest jewel they bring from thence is their maypole (say rather than stinking poole), which they bring home with great veneration." This interesting passage lets us know that the old Pagan rites were confounded with witchcraft, and confirms the evidence that the persecution of witches was the last act in the tragic suppression of Paganism. The rites of May Day are in reality a continuation of the rites of Dionysus Sabazios. Mr. W. W. Story says: "Scarcely does the sun drop behind bonfires begin to blaze from all the country towns on the mountainsides, showing like great beacons. This is a custom founded in great antiquity, and common to the North and South. The

Rites of Dionysus.

first of May is the Festival of the Holy Apostles in Italy; but in Germany, it is *Walpurgisnacht*, when goblins, witches, hags and devils hold high holiday, mounting on their brooms for the Brocken."

In the Neapolitan towns great fires are built on this festival, around which people dance, jumping through the flames, and flinging themselves about in every wild and fantastic attitude. Similar bonfires may also be seen blazing everywhere over the hills, and on the Campagna on the eve of the day of San Giovanni, which occurs on the 24th June. These are relics of the old Pagan custom alluded to by Ovid,[1] and particularly described by Varro, when the peasants made huge bonfires of straw, hay, and other

---

[1] Anon leap with nimble feet and straining thews across the burning heaps of crackling straw.–*Fasti*, lib. 4, v. 781-2.

Witches out for a good time during Walpurgisnacht.

Dancing around bonfire.

flammable materials, called "*Palilia*," and men, women and children dance round them and leaped through them in order to obtain expiation and free themselves from evil influences–the mothers holding out over the flames those children who were too young to take an active part in this rite.

In the Roman martyrology, St. Walburga's Feast–a day that commemorates the date of her canonization–is on May 1, though it isn't celebrated liturgically on the 1962 calendar. Her Feast is, however, a great holiday in many European countries, especially in Germany, Finland, Sweden, and Eastern European countries, and the celebrations begin on its eve–the night of 30 April–a time known as Walpurgisnacht.

The Maypole dance.

The chief feature of May Day was setting up the maypole. This being the time when the sap rises in the oak, the priests, joining the people, used to go in procession to some adjoining wood on the May morning, and return in triumph with the much-prized pole, adorned with boughs, flowers, ribbons and others tokens of the spring season. Besides the principal maypole, others of less dimensions were likewise erected in our villages, to mark the places where refreshments were to be obtained: hence the name of *ale stake* is frequently to be met with in old authors, as signifying a maypole. Bishop Grosseteste (d. 1253) suppressed the May games in the diocese of Lincoln, because partaking of heathen vanity; and from that period and example the practices of the day have gradually altered from their original mode of celebration. Stubbes remarks that when the maypole was reared, "they fall to banquet and feast, to leap and dance about it, as the heathen people did at the dedication of their idols, whereof this is a perfect pattern, or, rather, the thing itself." The acrid old Puritan was quite right. The maypole was an emblem of the life and generation manifest in the flowering of vegetation. It was the symbol of the renewal of life, as was also Flora, or our Maid Marian, or the Queen of the May; while Jack-in-the-Green represents the tree spirit, whose role is so important in all the old religions.

The last maypole in London was taken down in 1718. It was set up in Wanstead Park, Essex, as a support to Sir Isaac Newton's large telescope. Pope thus perpetuates its remembrance:–

Green Man.

"Amidst the area wide they took their stand,
Where the tall maypole o'erlook'd the Strand."

"The Mayings," says Trutt, in his *Sports and Pastimes*, 1801, "are in some sort yet kept up by the milkmaids at London, who go about the streets with their garlands and music, dancing." But the milkmaids gave place to the chimney-sweeps, as Maid Marian had to Malkin, a clown dressed in woman's clothes; and even the sooty sweeps have almost entirely abandoned the festival. Our country largely owned its title of "Merrie England" to its remnants of Paganism. Puritanism did much towards stamping these out, but Puritanism has in turn itself become almost as effete as Paganism.

Had the Puritans known the *Pervigilium Veneris*, a Latin poem ascribed by Erasmus to Catullus, but certainly later, it would have afforded them an additional text for invective against the Pagan superstitions which the May games were denounced as representing. The poem shows that the Romans, like our English ancestors, celebrated the season by betaking themselves to the woods for three nights, where they kept vigil in honour of Venus, to whom the month of April was dedicated, as

Venus

being the universal generating and producing power. The poem seems to have been composed with a view to its being sung by a choir of maidens in their nocturnal rambles beneath the soft light of an Italian moon. All the signs of spring whisper of love, and the constant refrain comes in, *Cras amet, qui nunquam amavit; quique amavit, cras amet.* Students of peasant customs and mythology will not be surprised at the suggestion that the three nights of vigil arose from watching the seeds which were expected to sprout at this season within three days.

May is the month of Mary, the mother of God, as it formerly was of Cybele, mother of the gods, the Bona Dea of the ancient Romans, whose feast at this period naturally associated itself with that of Flora. A remnant of the Foralia is preserved in the *Infiorata*

Cybele

or flower festival, dedicated now to the Madonna dei Fiori, celebrated every May at Genzano, which lies over the old crater now filled by the still waters of Lake Nemi. All the people are gaily dressed, and fun and flowers prevail, and as night comes on the young people dance the salterello in the very groves where the *Rex Nemorensis* obtained his office by slaying his predecessor.

The Infiorata, flower festival murals, like giant carpets on the street, are created with flowers.

The Infiorata takes place in May every year.

CHAPTER FOUR
CHRISTMAS

"At Christmas play and make good cheer,
For Christmas comes but once a year."
       TUSSER, *Five Hundred Points
       of Good Husbandry,* chap. xii.

"Heigh ho! sing, heigh ho!
  unto the green holly;
Most friendship is feigning,
  most loving mere folly.
Then heigh ho, the holly,
This life is most jolly."
            —*As You Like It,* Act ii. sc. I.

"The Roman winter-solstice festival, as celebrated on December 25 (viii. Kal. Jan.) in connection with the worship of the sun-god Mithra, appears to have been instituted in this special form after the Easter campaign of Aurelian, A.D. 273, and to this festival the day owes it apposite name of Birthday of the Unconquered Sun, *Die Natalis Solis invicti*. With full symbolic appropriateness, though not with historical justification, the day was adopted in the Western Church, where it appears to have been generally introduced by the fourth century, and when in time it passed to the Eastern Church, as the solemn anniversary of the birth of Christ, the Christian *Dies Natalis*–Christmas Day. Attempts have been made to ratify this date as matter of history, but no valid nor even consistent early Christian tradition vouches for it. The real solar origin of the festival is clear from the writings of the Fathers after its institution. In religious symbolism of the material and spiritual sun, Augustine and Gregory of Nyssa discourse on the glowing light and dwindling darkness that follow the Nativity; while Leo the Great, among whose people the earlier solar meaning of the festival evidently remained in strong remembrance, rebuked in a sermon the pestiferous persuasion, as he calls it, that this solemn day is to be honoured, not for the birth of Christ, but for the rising, as they say, of the new sun."

–E.B. TYLOR, *Primitive Culture*, Vol. II., pp. 297, 298.

The Christian institution of our principal festival is best stated in the words of St. Chrysostom (Hom., xxxi.): "On this day the birthday of Christ was *lately* fixed at Rome, in order that while the heathens were occupied in their profane ceremonies the Christians might perform their holy rites undisturbed. But they call this day 'the Birthday of the Invincible One [Mithra].' Who is so invincible as the Lord that overthrew and vanquished Death? Or because they style it the 'Birthday of the Sun.' He is the Sun of Righteousness, of whom Malachi saith, "Upon you, fearful ones, the Sun of Righteousness shall arise with healing in his wings."

Mithra the sun god.

The only connection between jolly Father Christmas and the young man of sorrows, said to have come to an untimely end in Jerusalem, is a church-made one. On the face of it Christmas is a Pagan festival. The head of the house, who invites his scattered family to make merry with him at this time,

Father Christmas with Yule log.

does exactly what his Pagan ancestors did centuries before the Christian era. Nor has the strong arm of religion quite banished the Pagan name, for in many parts Yuletide and Yule log and glad Yule are still favorite terms. Yule signifies the revolution of the year.

The hauling home of the Yule log and lighting it from a remnant of last year's log, the custom down to modern times, was the survival of the ever-burning house fire; and takes us back to the early times when, in the words of Max Müller, "the hearth was the first altar, the father the first elder, his wife

Hauling home the Yule log and the Yule jester.

and children and slaves the first congregation, gathered together round the sacred fire." The Yule festival was celebrated by the Druids with great fires lighted on the tops of the hills.

The venerable Bede says (da Rat. Temp., xiii) that in England the heathen inhabitants celebrated this very time. "They began," he says, "their year on the 8th of the Calends of January [25th December], which is now our Christmas Day; and the very night before, which is now holy to us, was by them called Maedrenack, or the Night of Mothers; because (as we imagine) of those ceremonies which were performed that night." The days at this time just beginning to lengthen, the Mother night was held to give them birth. The women took part in a nocturnal watch, now generally transferred to New Year's eve.

To get back to the origin of Christmas, we must put ourselves in the place of men who had no clear conception of the uniformity of

Night of Mothers.

natural law, and to whom, when winter with its long gloomy nights came, killing off vegetation, the question of questions was, when would brighter seasons return? Evergreens which told of the vitality of nature would be honoured, and the first assurance of the longer day hailed with acclamation.

Evergreens represented nature's vitality.

The Northern nations looked with special interest on the conflict of light and darkness. The passing of the period of the shortest day is the renewal of hope, the birthday of the Saviour. Before Christians brought their superstitions to these islands the inhabitants celebrated the return of the lighter days with a festival of rejoicing. The mistletoe is a Druidical emblem. The Yule log goes back to our Pagan forefathers. These show a solar character, as did likewise the bonfires lighted at Midsummer of St. John's Day. How appropriately does the genius of Midsummer, St. John, say of the genius of Christmas: "He must increase, but I must decrease," as the days begin to lengthen from December 25, and to shorten from June 24, till they reach the shortest, of which the genius saint is the unbelieving Thomas, standing in all the darkness of unbelief as to whether the Lord will rise again. In the Christmas service chant, *"Sol novus oritur,"* we see the adaptation of ancient solar thought to Christian allegory.

When Christianity spread through the Roman Empire it found everywhere among the heathen a festival to the sun-god, or the general spirit of life and vegetation celebrated at the winter solstice. From December 21 till the end of the year the Romans held the Saturnalia, a season marked by the universal prevalence of license and merry-making. Temporary freedom was given to slaves.

Saturnalia

Everyone feasted and rejoiced, work and business were for a season entirely suspended, the houses were decked with laurel and evergreen, visits and presents were exchanged between friends, and clients gave gifts to their patrons. The whole season was one of rejoicing and goodwill, and all kinds of amusements were indulged in by the people (see Chambers' *Book of Days*). In the now extinct Lord of Misrule, and schoolboys "barring out," may be traced a remnant of the Saturnalia.

Lord of Misrule.

Some also think," says Bingham, "that the very design of appointing the feast of Christ's Nativity and Epiphany at this season of the year, was chiefly to oppose the vanities and excesses which the heathen indulged themselves in, upon their Saturnalia and Calends of January at this very time of the year." Precisely so.

The Puritans saw that Christmas was a remnant of Paganism, and when in power during the Long Parliament did their best to suppress the festival. Earcropped Prynne, in his *Histrio-Mastix*, lets out in fine style: "If we compare our Bacchanalian Christmases and New Year's Tides with these Saturnalia and Feast of Janus, we shall find such near affinity between them both in regard of time (they being both in the end of December and the first of January) and in their manner of solemnizing (both of them being spent in revelling, epicurism, wantonness, idleness, dancing, drinking, stage plays, masques, and carnal pomp and jollity), that we must needs conclude the one to be but the very ape or issue of the other." But Christmas was too strong for the Puritans, and at the Restoration of the old festival was celebrated with new vigour.

Dancing, drinking, and idleness.

The custom of decorating houses with evergreens, evident symbols of life continued through the dead of winter, prevailed long anterior to Christianity. The Christian Father Tertullian, early in the third century affirmed it to be "rank idolatry" to deck their doors "with garlands or flowers on festival days according to the custom of the heathen." Polydore-Vergil says, "the decorating of temples with hangings of flowers, boughs, and garlands, was adopted from the Pagan nations, who decked their houses and temples in a similar manner." The Christmas tree, derived from our Teutonic forefathers, and carried through the world whatever Teutons go, with its fruit of good things for the little ones, is another sign of faith in returning spring and harvest. The mistletoe was regarded by the Druids as the seed which carried over vegetative life from the old year to the new. Hence, to kiss, and pluck a seed, was a sign of life and fertility.

Father Tertullian

Druids gathering mistletoe.

The infant Christ is as much a symbol of the returning year as the holly or the Christmas tree. The birthday of Christ is the birthday of the new year. Just as they now sing carols to the new born king, so, in ancient times, they sang carols to the vegetation itself, of which Shakespeare's "Heigh-ho the holly" is a remnant. In the North they carry round the infant Christ with his mother. In English villages this used to be the custom. Girls carried a wax doll in a box surrounded with evergreen and fruits. Whoever gave them money took a leaf which, carefully preserved, brought luck. This was good tidings of great joy, so that there was a proverb, "As unhappy as the man who has seen no advent images." So bakers would bake Yule doughs or little images, with currants for eyes, which were presented to their customers. These were intended as images of the new born King, and it was believed that he who preserved his Yule dough unbroken all through the year would not be injured by fire or water or slain by the sword.

The infant Christ

Barnaby Googe thus refers to the old midnight mass:–

> "Then comes the day wherein the Lord did bring
> his birth to passe;
> Whereas at midnight up they rise and every man to
> masse.
> This time so holy counted is, that divers, earnestly,
> Do think the waters all to wine are changed
> suddenly
> In that same hour that Christ Himself was born
> and came to light,
> And unto water strait again transformed and
> altered quite.
> There are beside that mindfully the money still
> do watch;
> That first to the altar comes which they privately
> do snatch.
> The priests, lest others should have it, take often
> the same away,
> Whereby they think, throughout the year, to have
> good luck in play,
> And not to lose. Then strait at game till daylight do
> they strive
> To make some present proof how well their
> hallowed pence will thrive."

That is to say, they first stole the money from the altar, and then began to gamble with it in church to prove its virtue as protecting them from loss. In South America, to this day, they hold a cock-crowing mass on Christmas. The young people at midnight interrupt the priest with cock-crowings and shouting, and after they leave the church spend the time in revelry. Googe thus refers to the masses on Christmas Day:–

> "Three masses every priest doth sing upon that solemn day
> With offerings unto every one that so the more may play.
> This done, a wooden child in clothes is on the altar set,
> About the which both boys and girls do dance and trimly jet
> And carols sing in praise of Christ, and for to help them hear
> The organs answer every verse, with sweet and solemn cheer.
> The priests do roar aloud; and round about the parents stand,
> To see the sport, and with their voice do help them and their band.

On Christmas morning, before break of day, the greatest uproar prevailed through a great number of boys going round from house to house, rapping at every door, and roaring out, "I wish you a merry Christmas and a happy New Year" which words were vociferated again and again, till the family was aroused, and the clamorous visitors were admitted. Cole (*Hist. and Antiq. of Filey* p. 137) says: "The first who came were treated with money, gingerbread and cheese, which are distributed to all on the Christmas

"Happy New Year" shout the little boys.

morning, but less liberally than to the first comers. No person, boys excepted, dared presume to go out of doors till the threshold had been consecrated by the entrance of a male. Females had no part in this matter, for although a lady were as fair as an angel, her form would be viewed as prognostic of death, were she the first to cross the threshold on Christmas morning." These customs of first footing and lucky-birding are now transferred to the New Year.

In Yorkshire children still go vessel cupping–as they call going round with the box containing Christmas dolls, or images taken from the mantelpiece. "Please may we sing you the 'Vessel-cup'" they say; but instead

Wassail-cup

of singing the Wassail-cup, they sing a Christmas carol. The box in old times would sometimes contain a cup instead of dolls. Drinking from the wassail bowl was a pledge of health and fortune. In some places still the wassailing of orchards, pouring beer or cider on the roots of trees at Christmas is still maintained, a venerable fragment of tree-worship. It was the custom in Devonshire, and probably in other countries also, to perform the following ceremonial on Christmas Eve. In the evening the farmer's family and friends being assembled, hot wheat-flour cakes were introduced, with cider. This was served round, the cake being dipped in the cider and then eaten. As the evening wore on, the company adjourned to the orchard, some bearing hot cake and cider as an offering to the principal tree; the cake was deposited on a fork up the tree, and the cider thrown over it, the men firing off muskets, fowling pieces, pistols, etc. In Norfolk they sprinkled spiced ale over the orchards and meadows, and the New Forest they mixed apples with the drink, singing:–

"Apples and pears with right good corn
Come in plenty to every one,
Eat and drink, good cake and ale
Give Earth to drink; and she'll not fail."

Eating the boar's head was a symbol of the triumph over winter. The old Oxford carol, "The boar is dead," explains the symbol:–

"The boar is dead,
 So here's his head,
   What man could have
   done more
 Than his head off to strike.
 Meleager like,
   And bring it as I do before?

"He living spoiled
 Where good men toiled
   Which made kind Ceres sorry'
 But now dead and drawn
 Is very good brawn,
   And we have brought it for ye.

"Then set down the swine yard,
 The foe to the vineyard,
   Let Bacchus crown his fall.
 Let this boar's head and mustard
 Stand for pig, goose, and custard,
   And so ye are welcome all."

In the Odin Religion as Carlyle tells us in his article in the *Westminster Review*, October, 1854, "Freir rode on a golden-bristled boar, *Gullinburste*; his festival was held at the turn of the year, at Yuletide; and is still commemorated in that season at Oxford and other places, where 'the procession of the boar's head,' Freir's symbol, is solemnized at Christmas time; a custom really venerable, considering how far down it has travelled on the road of ages!"

The procession of the boar.

Plum puddings and mince pies are not, as Brady says, "In token of the offerings of the wise men from the East," but representative sacraments. They are compounds of the good things of the past season, partaking which would ensure prosperity for that ensuing. Hence the saying, as many pieces of pudding or mince-pie are partaken, so many happy months. As the communion was originally taken by all the clan, to this may be traced the family reunions at the present day.

Pantomimes are associated with Christmas; and because the harlequinade is of Italian origin some think they are quite modern.

Italian Harlequin

I hold that this and the common view that the drama has grown from the miracle plays of the Middle Ages is wrong. It has been so usual to ascribe everything to the Church, and this theory has been supposed to reflect such credit upon the stage, that it has been allowed to pass unchallenged. Yet I am convinced this is a mistake. The Christmas pantomimes have developed from the court masques performed at Christmas, and these again from the Yuletide mummers, who were long anterior to the miracle plays. In Ben Johnson's :Christmas, his Masque," two of the characters are taken by Minced Pie and Bride Cake, as in Shakespeare's "Midsummer Night's Dream," we have the per-

Christmas mummers

sonal representation not only of a lion and a wall, but of moonshine. This takes us back to the old idea of mummery, which was that of imitative magic. Both the Christmas mummers and the miracle plays, developed from a common source; the idea expressed in festival ceremonies of savages, the buffalo and other dances of North American Indians, and the carrying of the Bambino to child-bearing women; the notion that the representation of actions was a charm to realize them. The Christmas mummers wore the heads of animals. The principal characters of the harlequinade represent the four seasons. The harlequin with his magically changing wand is the spirit of spring. The gay dancing columbine is summer, the sausage-stuffing clown, autumn, and tottering pantaloon, winter. The clown also preserves features of the lord of misrule and abbot of unreason, a character probably derived from the temporary kings, and earlier than Christianity.

The following act of a "pageant" which took place at Christmas 1410 is extracted from the "Records of Norwich," and throws light on the character of the festival. "John Hadman, a wealthy citizen, made disport with his neighbors and friends, and was crowned King of Christmas. He rode in state through the city, dressed forth in silks and tinsel, and preceded by twelve persons as the twelve months of the year." The Records continue: "After King Christmas, followed Lent, clothed in white garments trimmed with herring skins, on horseback, the horse

King of Christmas

being decorated with trappings of oyster shells, being indicative that sadness and a holy time should follow Christmas revelling.

In this way they rode through the city, accompanied by numbers in various grotesque dresses, making disport and merriment, some

Devils chasing revellers.

clad in armor; others dressed as devils chased the people, and sorely affrighted the women and children; others wearing skin dresses and counterfeiting bears, wolves, lions, and other animals, and endeavoring to imitate the animals they represented, in roaring and raving, alarming the cowardly and appalling the stoutest hearts."

Stow in his *Survey* (38) says: "At the feast of Christmas there was in the king's house, wheresoever he was lodged, a Lord of Misrule, or Master of merry disports, and the like had ye in the house of honour or good worship, were he spiritual or temporal. Amongst the which the Mayor of London, and either of the sheriffs, had their several Lords of Misrule, ever contending, without quarrel or offence, who should make the rarest pastimes to delight the beholders. These lords beginning their rule on All hallow Eve, continued the same till the morrow after the Feast of the Purification, commonly called Candlemas Day. In all which space there were fine and subtle disguises, masks, and mummeries, with playing at cards for counters, nails, and points, in every house, more for pastime than for gain." The lawyers also elected a Christmas lord, and they had the usual shows performed in their several Inns of Court. Their lord was up early in the morning hunting out his officers, and "pulling all the loiterers out of bed to make their early sport, but after breakfast the fun was suspended until the evening, when it was opened again day after day with great spirit until the holidays ended. The judges attended every evening, and the 'under barristers' were bound to dance before their lordships. On one occasion, when this was omitted, the whole bar was offended, and at Lincoln's Inn, the offenders were by decimation put out of commons for example's sake; and should the same omission be repeated, they were to be fined or disbarred; for these dances were thought necessary 'as much conducing to the making of gentlemen more fit for their books at other times.' "

When the old mysteries came to be adopted by the monks, they preserved some curious features. There is one called "The Miraculous Birth and the Midwives," the object of which is to exhibit the Nativity, and to hold up those to dishonor who ventures upon questioning the purity of Mary. It opens with a scene in which Joseph informs Mary that they must go up to Bethlehem to be taxed; but he fears to take her.

While they are on their journey, Mary espies a tree, and in answer to her question, Joseph informs her that it is a cherry tree. Alluding to her then condition, she asks him to pluck freely for her eating, and urges that she longs for some of its fruit. But Joseph says, "Let him pluck you cherries that gat you with child." Mary now prays to God to make the tree bow down so that she may pick for herself, and immediately her wish is granted.

Mary picking cherries.

When Joseph saw the tree bow, he humbled himself. Then follows the staying in the stable, the bringing in of midwives, who make speeches, and one of them–incredulous as Thomas–declares that the story of the other nurse, "that Mary is a virgin pure" cannot be true, for which she immediately loses the use of her arm, which falls "dead and dry." This alarms and convinces her, she prays for pardon, her arm is restored, and then she declares her resolve to publish the wondrous birth unto all men. With this the mystery terminates.

As kept up by the laity Christmas mumming usually preserved features of old nature worship. Father Christmas himself was a popular character, and St. George, the sun god, many of whose features are like those of

The Nativity and birth of Jesus.

Horus, was the head of the seven champions of Christendom, originally the seven days of the week. But the merest glance at Christmas customs should suffice to show that Christmas was not instituted to celebrate the birth of Jesus in Palestine at a time when shepherds could not watch their flocks by night, but Christ was said to have been born at the time of the winter solstice, since this was the Pagan season for celebrating the rebirth of the Sun.

Winter Solstice

New Falcon Publications
**Publisher of Controversial Books and CDs
Invites You to Visit Our Website:
http://www.newfalcon.com**

At the Falcon website you can:

- Browse the online catalog of all our great titles, including book by Robert Anton Wilson, Christopher S. Hyatt, Israel Regardie Aleister Crowley, Timothy Leary, Osho, Lon Milo DuQuette and many more
- Find out what's available and what's out of stock
- Get special discounts
- Order our titles through our secure online server
- Find products not available anywhere else including:
    - One of a kind and limited availability products
    - Special packages
    - Special pricing
- And much, much more

Get online today at http://www.newfalcon.com